Presented to

....

From

....

Wedding Date

....

Introduction

The big day is coming! As you plan and prepare, prayer will be more important than anything and everything else you do. Prayer will prepare you for the events and the new life coming. It will be a critical part of the firm foundation upon which God will continue to build and strengthen you. And to be frank, prayer will be the key to survival—through planning, the wedding, and life-ever-after.

This journal is designed to be used by brides or their mothers. The prayer excerpts are here to encourage your hearts as you plan and pray for the big day—whether it is your wedding or your daughter's. Bible verses are included on the journaling pages to speak truth into the planning stages of the wedding.

Let the verses and prayers inspire your own words of praise and petition as the big day approaches. Or use the pages to keep to-do lists, important notes and numbers, or a place to count the blessings of each day.

Congratulations! May God bless you, your planning, and the wedding.

The fear of the Lord is the beginning of wisdom; all who follow his precepts
have good understanding. To him belongs eternal praise.

PSALM 111:10

You were chosen according to the purpose of God the Father and were made
a holy people by his Spirit, to obey Jesus Christ and be purified by his blood.
May grace and peace be yours in full measure.

1 PETER 1:2 GNT

Do not be anxious about anything, but in every situation, by prayer and petition, with thanksgiving, present your requests to God. And the peace of God, which transcends all understanding, will guard your hearts and your minds in Christ Jesus.

PHILIPPIANS 4:6-7

I have hidden your word in my heart that I might not sin against you.
PSALM 119:11

Bride's Prayer

Lord, I pray that wherever You lead us, we would hear Your voice and follow. Whenever we get discouraged, remind us that Your plans for our life together cannot be thwarted. Help us to know that we are never alone. You walk with us, one step and one breath at a time as we accomplish Your will. Lord, help me to respect, support, and trust my future spouse; help me believe that You have a perfect plan for our lives. Where You lead us, we will follow.

You, Lord, are good, and ready to forgive, and abundant in mercy
to all those who call upon You.

PSALM 86:5 NKJV

Cast your burden on the Lord, and he will sustain you;
he will never permit the righteous to be moved.

PSALM 55:22 ESV

Do not forsake wisdom, and she will protect you; love her, and she will watch over you.
The beginning of wisdom is this: Get wisdom. Though it cost all you have, get understanding.

PROVERBS 4:6-7

A good person produces good things from the treasury of a good heart....
What you say flows from what is in your heart.

Walk in a manner worthy of the calling to which you have been called,
with all humility and gentleness, with patience, bearing with one another in love,
eager to maintain the unity of the Spirit in the bond of peace.

EPHESIANS 4:1-3 ESV

Honor one another above yourselves.

ROMANS 12:10

This is what the Lord says—your Redeemer, the Holy One of Israel: "I am the Lord your God, who teaches you what is best for you, who directs you in the way you should go."

ISAIAH 48:17

Mother's Prayer

Father, today I pray that this couple's hearts and minds would be filled to overflowing with a greater understanding of the breadth and depth of Your boundless love. Bless them with an unrivaled intimacy with You that results in them experiencing love in such a profound way that they will never be the same.

Father, I pray that Your immeasurable, all-consuming love would define who they are in such a way that they will never have to search for love or satisfaction anywhere else. Because this young couple's hearts are filled to overflowing with *Your* love, I pray that *their* love would abound more and more in knowledge and depth of insight.

Our mouths were filled with laughter, our tongues with songs of joy.
Then it was said among the nations, "The Lord has done great things for them."
The Lord has done great things for us, and we are filled with joy.

Oh, the joys of those who do not follow the advice of the wicked, or stand around with sinners, or join in with mockers. But they delight in the law of the Lord, meditating on it day and night. They are like trees planted along the riverbank, bearing fruit each season. Their leaves never wither, and they prosper in all they do.

PSALM 1:1-3 NLT

Whoever wishes to save his life will lose it, but whoever
loses his life for My sake, he is the one who will save it.

LUKE 9:24 NASB

You, my brothers and sisters, were called to be free. But do not use your freedom to indulge the flesh; rather, serve one another humbly in love. For the entire law is fulfilled in keeping this one command: "Love your neighbor as yourself."

GALATIANS 5:13-14

Be strong and courageous. Do not be afraid or terrified...
for the Lord your God goes with you; he will never leave you nor forsake you.
DEUTERONOMY 31:6

I have told you these things, so that in me you may have peace. In this world you
will have trouble. But take heart! I have overcome the world.

JOHN 16:33

Remain in me, as I also remain in you. No branch can bear fruit by itself;
it must remain in the vine. Neither can you bear fruit unless you remain in me.
JOHN 15:4

Bride's Prayer

Lord, help me to trust You completely with everything regarding my wedding day and my marriage. From the smallest details to what matters most to me and everything in between, help me to trust You. But more importantly, please help me to trust You with my fiancé. He is Yours. And by Your amazing grace, You have entrusted him to me to love, honor, respect, and cherish all my days here on this earth. What a blessing! What a privilege! Heavenly Father, I do not take this responsibility lightly. I know that I cannot be the godly wife that he needs without You. Thank You, Lord, for providing everything I need to take care of my future husband and for trusting me with his heart.

That is why a man leaves his father and mother and is united to his wife,
and they become one flesh.
GENESIS 2:24

Heal me, Lord, and I will be healed; save me and I will be saved, for you are the one I praise.

JEREMIAH 17:14

I consider that our present sufferings are not worth comparing
with the glory that will be revealed in us.
ROMANS 8:18

So do not fear, for I am with you; do not be dismayed, for I am your God.
I will strengthen you and help you; I will uphold you with my righteous right hand.

ISAIAH 41:10

The Lord takes delight in his people; he crowns the humble with victory.

PSALM 149:4

The righteous lead blameless lives; blessed are their children after them.

PROVERBS 20:7

We will not hide these truths from our children; we will tell the next generation about the glorious deeds of the Lord, about his power and his mighty wonders.

PSALM 78:4 NLT

Mother's Prayer

Father, I am so grateful that You are trustworthy. I can trust You completely, no matter what. My prayer is that this couple would trust You and trust each other implicitly. Help them to take the risks necessary to trust each other in every area of their relationship. Help them to be intentional and vulnerable—with hearts wide open! Give them the grace to sincerely and honestly communicate, to show compassion, and to truly understand one another. Don't let the sun go down on their anger, Lord; help them be quick to hear, slow to speak, and slow to get angry. Give them the grace to be forgiving when the other is hurtful or careless with their words.

We know that in all things God works for the good of those who love him,
who have been called according to his purpose.

ROMANS 8:28

Devote yourselves to prayer, being watchful and thankful.
COLOSSIANS 4:2

The Word became flesh and made his dwelling among us. We have seen his glory,
the glory of the one and only Son, who came from the Father, full of grace and truth.
JOHN 1:14

Give thanks in all circumstances; for this is God's will for you in Christ Jesus.
1 THESSALONIANS 5:18

A gentle answer turns away wrath, but a harsh word stirs up anger.

PROVERBS 15:1

May the God who gives patience, steadiness, and encouragement help you to live
in complete harmony with each other—each with the attitude of Christ toward the other.
And then all of us can praise the Lord together with one voice, giving glory to God,
the Father of our Lord Jesus Christ.

ROMANS 15:5-6 TLB

Therefore what God has joined together, let no one separate.

MARK 10:9

Bride's Prayer

Father, 1 Thessalonians 5:18 tells us to be thankful in everything, because that's Your will for us. Lord, if it's Your will that we be thankful in all circumstances, give us the courage to do so, because life is hard. We all experience pain and heartache, and oftentimes, giving thanks is the last thing we want to do. But regardless of the struggles, You are still God, and You are still good, all the time. Being thankful is not about how we feel in any given situation; it's about choosing to love and obey You and Your will for our lives. So, Lord, regardless of how we feel or what's going on in our lives, please help both of us to be thankful, no matter what.

Nobody should seek his own good, but the good of others.

1 CORINTHIANS 10:24

Commit your works to the Lord and your plans will be established.
PROVERBS 16:3 NASB

We love because he first loved us.

1 JOHN 4:19

All things are done according to God's plan and decision; and God chose us
to be his own people in union with Christ because of his own purpose,
based on what he had decided from the very beginning.

EPHESIANS 1:11 GNT

This is the confidence we have in approaching God: that if we ask anything according to his will, he hears us.

The word of God is alive and active. Sharper than any double-edged sword,
it penetrates even to dividing soul and spirit, joints and marrow;
it judges the thoughts and attitudes of the heart.

HEBREWS 4:12

Blessed is the one who trusts in the Lord, whose confidence is in him. They will be like a tree planted by the water that sends out its roots by the stream. It does not fear when heat comes; its leaves are always green. It has no worries in a year of drought and never fails to bear fruit.

JEREMIAH 17:7-8

Mother's Prayer

Father, thank You for creating us on purpose for a purpose. I ask with all my heart that this precious couple would bravely pursue Your call, knowing that Your plans for them are always good. And if that call leads them beyond their comfort zones, I pray that they would have the courage, faith, and strength to move onward and upward in pursuit of Your call on their lives.

God, they cannot pursue a call they are unaware or unsure of. Please give them wisdom and clarity—let their hearts hear and know Your voice above the clamor and chaos of the many voices that vie for their attention. Bless them with the faith to stay committed to You and Your call.

Give thanks in all circumstances; for this is God's will for you in Christ Jesus.

1 THESSALONIANS 5:18

I am convinced that neither death nor life, neither angels nor demons, neither the present nor the future, nor any powers, neither height nor depth, nor anything else in all creation, will be able to separate us from the love of God that is in Christ Jesus our Lord.

ROMANS 8:38-39

Words kill, words give life; they're either poison or fruit—you choose.

PROVERBS 18:21 MSG

To this you were called, because Christ suffered for you,
leaving you an example, that you should follow in his steps.

Turn my heart towards your statutes and not toward selfish gain.
Turn my eyes away from worthless things; preserve my life according to your word.
PSALM 119:36-37

Take my yoke upon you and learn from me, for I am gentle and humble in heart, and you will find rest for your souls. For my yoke is easy and my burden is light.

MATTHEW 11:29-30

Keep your lives free from the love of money and be content with what you have, because God has said, "Never will I leave you; never will I forsake you."

HEBREWS 13:5

Bride's Prayer

Heavenly Father, as my fiancé and I prepare for our wedding, please bless us with wisdom and understanding so that we can know You better. As every day draws us one day closer to the big day, please give us greater knowledge of the depths of Your love, goodness, and sovereignty. We have so many decisions to make, but You know exactly what we need. We cannot do this without You, so please, intervene and give us clarity. Father, I pray that everything leading up to our wedding—every meeting, every decision, every prayer—would be accomplished through the wisdom You freely give us.

But seek first his kingdom and his righteousness,
and all these things will be given to you as well.
MATTHEW 6:33

Give, and it will be given to you. A good measure, pressed down,
shaken together and running over, will be poured into your lap.
For with the measure you use, it will be measured to you.

LUKE 6:38

Now the Lord is the Spirit, and where the Spirit of the Lord is, there is freedom.

2 CORINTHIANS 3:17

My flesh and my heart may fail, but God is the strength of my heart and my portion forever.

PSALM 73:26

The Lord is gracious and righteous; our God is full of compassion.
The Lord protects the unwary; when I was brought low, he saved me.

PSALM 116:5-6

The fruit of the Spirit is love, joy, peace, forbearance, kindness, goodness, faithfulness, gentleness and self-control. Against such things there is no law.

GALATIANS 5:22-23

Let us not become weary in doing good, for at the proper time
we will reap a harvest if we do not give up.

GALATIANS 6:9

Mother's Prayer

Heavenly Father, I pray that this couple would be joyful always and laugh often. In those moments when life seems mundane and monotonous, please help them to appreciate and cherish the moments when they get to laugh out loud together. Every good and perfect gift comes from You, Lord. Bless this beloved couple with a sense of humor that honors You. Keep them from taking life too seriously and becoming overly dramatic and analytical. As often as possible, please bless them with the gift of a deep belly laugh, the kind of laughter that sets tears rolling down their cheeks.

Then they cried out to the Lord in their trouble, and he saved them from their distress.
He sent forth his word and healed them; he rescued them from the grave.

And the God of all grace, who called you to his eternal glory in Christ, after you have suffered a little while, will himself restore you and make you strong, firm and steadfast.

1 PETER 5:10

Every good and perfect gift is from above, coming down from the Father
of the heavenly lights, who does not change like shifting shadows.

The Lord will fight for you; you need only to be still.

EXODUS 14:14

Therefore, since we are surrounded by such a great cloud of witnesses, let us throw off everything that hinders and the sin that so easily entangles. And let us run with perseverance the race marked out for us, fixing our eyes on Jesus, the pioneer and perfecter of faith. For the joy set before him he endured the cross, scorning its shame, and sat down at the right hand of the throne of God.

HEBREWS 12:1-2

Remain in me, as I also remain in you. No branch can bear fruit by itself;
it must remain in the vine. Neither can you bear fruit unless you remain in me.
I am the vine; you are the branches. If you remain in me and I in you,
you will bear much fruit; apart from me you can do nothing.

JOHN 15:4-5

Jesus answered, "I am the way and the truth and the life.
No one comes to the Father except through me."

Bride's Prayer

Lord, before I was born, You orchestrated every detail in my life to bring me to this moment. You have been strategically and purposefully preparing my heart, mind, and body in every way. Heavenly Father, help me be keenly aware of Your presence on my wedding day. Fill me to overflowing with Your love so that nothing and no one can steal my joy. Help me be fully present so I can take it all in and enjoy and appreciate every moment. Please protect my mind and heart from distractions so that I can fully receive every blessing You have prepared for me.

All Scripture is God-breathed and is useful for teaching, rebuking, correcting and training in righteousness, so that the servant of God may be thoroughly equipped for every good work.

2 TIMOTHY 3:16-17

Whatever you do, whether in word or deed, do it all in the name of the Lord Jesus,
giving thanks to God the Father through him.

Do everything without grumbling or arguing, so that you may become blameless and pure, children of God without fault in a warped and crooked generation. Then you will shine among them like stars in the sky as you hold firmly to the word of life.

PHILIPPIANS 2:14-16

Not to us, Lord, not to us but to your name be the glory, because of your love and faithfulness.

Neither height nor depth, nor anything else in all creation, will be able to separate us
from the love of God that is in Christ Jesus our Lord.

ROMANS 8:39

This is love: not that we loved God, but that he loved us and sent his Son
as an atoning sacrifice for our sins.

1 JOHN 4:10

So whether you eat or drink or whatever you do, do it all for the glory of God.

1 CORINTHIANS 10:31

Mother's Prayer

Lord, in the face of fearful circumstances, it takes courage to pray and wait. We wait for You to do what only You can do. When my daughter and her husband-to-be are tempted to take matters into their own hands, please remind them to seek You and wait for wisdom, guidance, and direction. You see the big picture and how all the pieces of our lives fall into place. Help them to be patient and trust that in Your perfect timing, You will move on their behalf and work all things together for good.

About the Authors

JILL KELLY is a *New York Times* best-selling author, event speaker, and the wife of retired Buffalo Bills quarterback and pro football hall of famer Jim Kelly. Jill and Jim have three children—Erin, 23 years old, Hunter (February 14, 1997–August 5, 2005), and Camryn, 19 years old. As founder and chairman of the board of Hunter's Hope Foundation, Jill helps children with Krabbe Leukodystrophy and their families by extending the hope and comfort she has received through her relationship with Christ.

ERIN KELLY-BEAN is a *New York Times* best-selling author, event speaker, and the oldest daughter of Jill Kelly and her husband, retired Buffalo Bills quarterback and pro football hall of famer Jim Kelly. Erin has an inter-disciplinary degree in digital media and strategic communications from Liberty University. She is currently attending Liberty University School of Law. Erin is a member of the board for Hunter's Hope Foundation. She lives with her husband, Parker, and their dog, Blu, in Lynchburg, Virginia.

Ellie Claire® Gift & Paper Expressions
Franklin, TN 37067
EllieClaire.com
Ellie Claire is a registered trademark of Worthy Media, Inc.

Mother & Bride Prayer Journal
© 2018 by Jill Kelly and Erin Kelly-Bean
Published by Ellie Claire, an imprint of Worthy Publishing Group, a division of Worthy Media, Inc.

ISBN 978-1-633262-08-9

Unless otherwise noted, all Scriptures are taken from The Holy Bible, New International Version®, NIV®
Copyright © 1973, 1978, 1984, 2011 by Biblica, Inc.® All rights reserved worldwide. Other Scriptures are taken from
The Holy Bible, English Standard Version® (ESV®), copyright © 2001 by Crossway Bibles, a publishing ministry
of Good News Publishers. The New American Standard Bible® (NASB), Copyright © 1960, 1962, 1963, 1968, 1971,
1972, 1973, 1975, 1977, 1995 by The Lockman Foundation. Good News Translation (GNT)
Copyright © 1992 by American Bible Society. The New King James Version® (NKJV). Copyright © 1982
by Thomas Nelson. The Holy Bible, New Living Translation (NLT) copyright © 1996, 2004, 2007 by Tyndale House
Foundation. Used by permission of Tyndale House Publishers Inc., Carol Stream, Illinois 60188. *The Message* (MSG).
Copyright © 1993, 1994, 1995, 1996, 2000, 2001, 2002. Used by permission of NavPress Publishing Group.
The Living Bible (TLB) copyright © 1971 by Tyndale House Foundation. Used by permission of Tyndale House
Publishers Inc., Carol Stream, Illinois 60188. Used by permission. All rights reserved.

Stock or custom editions of Ellie Claire titles may be purchased in bulk for educational, business, ministry,
fundraising, or sales promotional use. For information, please e-mail info@EllieClaire.com

Published in association with Jana Burson of The Christopher Ferebee Agency, ChristopherFerebee.com.

Compiled by Jill Jones
Cover and interior art by iStock
Cover design by Melissa Reagan
Interior design by Bart Dawson

Printed in China
1 2 3 4 5 6 7 8 9 – 23 22 21 20 19 18